1.0   Introduction

We examine the efficacy of two policies introduced by the Federal Reserve designed to reinforce its commitment to an accommodative monetary policy in the aftermath of the financial crisis. In August 2011, the Federal Open Market Committee (FOMC) first provided date-based guidance on the anticipated minimum amount of time that it expected the federal funds rate, and hence other short-term interest rates, would remain at an extraordinarily low level (which we refer to as the guidance period). Under the Maturity Extension Program (MEP), first announced in September 2011, the Federal Reserve sold Treasury issues maturing within three years and purchased securities with more than six years to maturity. The overlapping guidance and MEP periods were marked by low and stable interest rates, increases in the inventories of Treasury securities of large financial intermediaries, and expectations of a continuation of accommodative monetary policy.

Although the two policies were geared toward accommodating policy, they created offsetting pressures on short-term interest rates. In the context of the literature on recent Federal Reserve policies, MEP securities sales did not signal a change in the future federal funds rate target but would have induced increases in short-term interest rates through changes in the composition of private sector portfolios. In contrast, the FOMC's date-based guidance for the federal funds rate explicitly signaled a low path of overnight interest rates with no obvious effect on the composition of private sector holdings. Here we examine the resulting market impact on rates, primary dealer inventories, and expectations from these two policies.

Of interest from an empirical perspective, the guidance timeframes were not the same as the maturity ranges of MEP sales. The asynchronous policy windows provide an opportunity for identification of program-specific effects at the boundary of guidance periods. Some of the securities sold through MEP, for example, had maturity dates that were inside the guidance period while others had maturity dates well beyond the end of particular guidance period. In this paper, we disentangle these program effects and conclude that each of the policies were effective in influencing interest rates of securities with the maturities directly affected and the interest rates of securities with maturities of longer than the stated policy dates.

The MEP and guidance policies together offer insights into the effectiveness of different mechanisms for the transmission of monetary policy since both policies were reserve neutral.[1] Proceeds from MEP sales were used to purchase Treasuries with longer maturities and interest rate guidance policies have been designed to influence interest rates without changing the size or composition of the Federal Reserve balance sheet.[2] The effectiveness of a guidance policy depends on central bank credibility while the effectiveness of the MEP primarily depends on the positive economic effects of any lowering of long term interest rates overwhelming any increase in short rates that occurs as a result of sales. Forward guidance might offset the impact of the MEP over the short end of the yield curve.

We analyze three sets of data related to short term financial markets that should have been affected by the Federal Reserve policies of 2011 and 2012. Section 2 provides background. Data and methods are described in section 3. In section 4, we provide and discuss results of our analysis and, in section 5, we provide brief concluding remarks.

We find that the date-based guidance was effective, not only in setting expectations for short term interest rates over the period stated by the FOMC but also for longer term interest rates. This effectiveness, however, did not fully buffer short-term Treasury securities from higher interest rates during the MEP.

2.0 Background

This background offers both a literature review and some detail on particulars of policy and markets over the period of study.

2.1 Federal Reserve Policy Actions in 2011 and 2012

Over this period, we examine five Federal Reserve policies that had the potential to affect short term interest rates. First, on August 9, 2011 the FOMC announced its expectations that the federal funds rate would remain exceptionally low through mid-2013. Guidance on FOMC rate

---

[1] Hrung and Seligman 2011 show that reserve neutral policies can be effective monetary policy tools. That paper focuses on two other programs employed by the Federal Reserve and Treasury in the wake of the financial crisis, the Federal Reserve s System's Term Securities Lending Facility program and the joint Treasury-Federal Reserve Supplemental Financing Program.

[2] Campbell et al (2012) study the impact of FOMC guidance over 2008 – 2012, finding impacts for market expectations. Glenn, Rudebush and Williams (2008) give background on the evolution of forward guidance over time.

policy was extended to late-2014 on January 25, 2012 and to mid-2015 on September 13, 2012.[3] The initial guidance, following the FOMC's August 2011 meeting, stated:

> *The Committee currently anticipates that economic conditions--including low rates of resource utilization and a subdued outlook for inflation over the medium run--are likely to warrant exceptionally low levels for the federal funds rate at least through mid-2013.*

Later guidance, in January 2012 and September 2012, lengthened the period of anticipated low short term rates until the end of 2014 and mid-2015 respectively using similar language. It is possible that market participants interpreted these statements as information about the FOMC's average projection of economic activity. If those projections differed materially from ones held by market participants ahead of guidance, statements may have altered expectations of economic activity which in turn affect projections of future interest rate paths. Alternatively, market participants may have viewed the statements as a commitment by the Federal Reserve to maintain low short rates through the specified period. If the statements altered economic projections, we would expect rates to fall when Federal Reserve projections were more pessimistic than average market projections. If the statements were viewed as a commitment device, we would expect rates to fall to the extent that market participants had priced in earlier expected increases in short rates. In either case we expect an inflection point at the end of the stated guidance period unless the statement language was fully anticipated by market participants.

The MEP was introduced in September of 2011, with an initial end date of June 30, 2012 and extended to the end of 2012 at the FOMC's June 2012 meeting. The MEP offset purchases of long-dated Treasury securities with sales of short-dated Treasury securities. The first statement, in September 2011, set a pace of $44 billion per month of purchases and sales to be conducted through June of 2012.

> *The Committee intends to purchase, by the end of June 2012, $400 billion of Treasury securities with remaining maturities of 6 years to 30 years and to sell an equal amount of Treasury securities with remaining maturities of 3 years or less.*

Eight days before the program would have terminated, on June 22, 2012, the FOMC announced a continuation of the program with slightly different maturity guidelines. In the initial program,

---

[3] Statements, minutes, press conferences, and supporting documents are at:
http://www.federalreserve.gov/monetarypolicy/fomccalendars.htm

the three-year eligibility rolled forward so that as securities with slightly more than three years to maturity aged they would become eligible for sales. In the continuation of the program, the three-year window was determined by securities that would be eligible at the end of the program and then sold throughout the program even though, in the early months, some securities had maturities greater than three years.

2.2   *Previous Studies of the Federal Reserve's Policies Affecting Treasury Yields during and after the Financial Crisis*

Previous attempts to quantify impacts of Federal Reserve policy actions to influence interest rates since 2008 have often employed event studies. This method is arguably less useful here because theory suggests that the effect of guidance announcements should be more continuous. In contrast to most of the literature on the Federal Reserve's efforts to stimulate the economy following the financial crisis, we focus on policies that should have affected the prices of short-dated securities. Bauer and Rudebusch (2012) put much of the emerging literature on long-dated securities in the context of the question of whether asset purchases by the Federal Reserve affect interest rates by changing the composition of private sector holdings (a "portfolio balance" effect) or by changing the expectations of market participants of the path of future short-term interest rates (a "signaling" effect). The guidance on the FOMC's expectations of the duration of low short-term interest rates is an unambiguous example of signaling.

While the sales of short-dated securities could be interpreted as a signal of future short-dated rates (for example if purchasers trust that the Federal Reserve would be unlikely to cause the prices of securities it has sold to fall), the most obvious effect is a portfolio balance one: financial market participants had to absorb new supplies of short-dated Treasury securities while parting with long-dated Treasury securities.[4]

Focusing on Federal Reserve actions in 2011 and 2012 allows us to study events in a relatively stable environment. The Federal Reserve's announcements during the financial crisis (particularly in late 2008 and 2009) are likely to have had large effects on interest rates by causing market participants to substantially alter their assessments of general market risk.[5] In contrast, we expect that the 2011-12 actions caused market participants to more narrowly alter

---

[4] Both academics and policymakers have tended to downplay the possible portfolio effects of the Treasury sales. The duration of securities sold was generally short and, from a policy perspective, may have rounded to zero.
[5] Studies of LSAP1 include Gagnon, Raskin, Remache and Sack (2012) and D'Amico and King (2012).

either their expectations of the path of future short term interest rates or their expectations of net supply of specific securities.

While preferred maturity habits have been assumed by some authors and FOMC members,[6] Krishnamurthy and Vissing-Jorgensen (2011) find no evidence that corporate bond investors changed their maturity preferences based on FOMC actions. They point to interacted issuer-duration channels as more important drivers of yield changes following FOMC announcements, emphasizing a "safety channel" that can be described as a preferred habitat. To incorporate preferred habitat behavior, recent papers have built on the work of Vayanos and Vila (2009) who modeled two groups of investors, one group that has maturity preferences and one group that arbitrages differences in yields across maturities.[7] The integration of preferred habitat investors with risk adverse arbitrageurs leads to empirically appealing results within a relatively simple modeling framework. While we do not explicitly model investor behavior, we find real effects from the Federal Reserve's sales of short-dated Treasury securities which, when considered with the purchases of similar quantities of long-dated Treasury securities, suggests validity for models like those of Vayanos and Vila.

FOMC transactions should have two sets of informational effects: an announcement or 'stock' effect that reflects market participants' initial assessments of the announced supply effect and an update or 'flow' effect that should reflect changes in expectations as the results of operations are made public. D'Amico and King (2012) examined the 2009 Federal Reserve purchases of Treasury securities and found the flow effects to be large but as (among others) Krishnamurthy and Vissing-Jorgensen point out, the change in interest rates on Treasury securities in 2009 reflected more than a simple adjustment of market participants' expectations of the impact of purchases. By using Primary Dealer position data, we consider how the flows associated with sales affected dealers' balance sheets.

We introduce indicator variables that explicitly address dealers' responses to MEP sales; so this work offers a more holistic perspective regarding the efficacy of these policies. This paper also differs from others looking at large scale transactions by the Federal Reserve in its focus on short-term securities, its explicit inclusion of related markets and its coverage of the interactions between sales and FOMC guidance.

---

[6] For example, Gagnon, Raskin, Remache and Sack (2010).
[7] For example, see Li and Wei (2012) and Hamilton and Wu (2012).

2.2 A brief aside on issuance of Treasury securities over the period of study

Through the period covered in this paper, the U.S. Treasury sold securities with maturities in the same range as the securities sold by the Federal Reserve. There were significant differences however, in the securities sold and the manner in which they were sold. The Treasury sells 2-year notes for month-end settlement and 3-year notes for mid-month settlement. These large sales are comprised of known quantities and known maturity dates. The sales are supported by a distribution infrastructure that includes pre-auction sales, price discovery ("when-issued" trading) and well-established uses as liquidity instruments. Of particular note, our task has been simplified by the Treasury; issuance amounts were unchanged throughout 2011 and 2012.

In contrast to Treasury, the Federal Reserve's MEP sales were, by construction much less uniform, as they were sales of securities already held by the Federal Reserve. Information was limited to an eligible set of securities that would be sold; the total amount being within an indicative dollar range. Uncertainty extended to the total amount of securities to be sold, the frequency of sales, and the particular securities included in each operation. In addition, participation was limited to the Federal Reserve Bank of New York's counterparties—by contrast Treasury sales are open to all market participants. We take up a more detailed discussion of data and method next.

3.0 Data and Methodology

The consequence of guidance and MEP sales should have led to a distinct difference in the interest rates on Treasury securities with maturities under three years. For securities with maturity dates before mid-2013, rates should have fallen on the August announcement and remained stable through the MEP announcement in September 2011. For securities with maturity dates beyond mid-2013 but shorter than July 2015, interest rates may have been brought down on the August announcement (based on higher valuations of shorter dated coupon payments) but should have risen following the September MEP announcement from the expected consequences of additional supply. The extension of the guidance on rates, announced in January 2012, should have put downward pressure on interest rates for securities maturing before the end of 2014. And, the MEP extension, announced in June 2012, should have put upward pressure on interest rates for securities maturing by January 2016. Table 1 documents our hypotheses (priors) regarding the expected effects of each announcement on securities of varying maturities.

<Table 1>

We consider the effects of sales and guidance on large standardized market rate: Treasury securities, overnight index swaps (OIS), and plain vanilla interest rate swaps. By looking across these markets, we can see the effectiveness of the transmission of the FOMC's guidance across markets and the potential transmission, presumably in the opposite direction, of the pressure from Treasury sales.

3.1 Data

Our interest rate data target relevant liquid maturity points (1-year, 2-year, 3-year, 4-year and 5-year) for short-dated securities.[8] The data cover the period from August 1, 2011 (just ahead of the first interest rate guidance announcement which occurred on August 9, 2012) through December 31, 2012, the end of the MEP policy period. Table 2 summarizes our data.

<Table 2 here>

Table 2 separates into three dependent variable clusters, the first targeting changes in U.S. Treasury rates, in absolute terms along the yield curve from which the Fed is offering securities for sale. The second group of dependent variables tracks the spread between Treasury and OIS rates over the same maturities and the last group tracks the Treasury-swap spread.

To assess the policy impacts on these dependent variables, we construct a series of policy coverage ratios that gauge the effects of non-standard monetary policies on interest rates. The coverage ratios are the percent of the constant maturity rate covered by either the guidance policy or the maturity range of sales of Treasury securities.[9]

For each maturity point on the yield curve, we construct controls for the guidance and MEP policies that reflect the degree of policy influence at each point in time. These controls

---

[8] For Treasury securities, we use zero coupon yields based Gurkaynak, Sack and Wright (2007) and publicly available at http://www.federalreserve.gov/pubs/feds/2006/200628/200628abs.html. OIS data are from Bloomberg. For interest rate swaps, we use rates published by the Federal Reserve at http://www.federalreserve.gov/releases/h15/data.htm. .

[9] For example, if the guidance period at date *t* was one full year, the 2-year coverage indicator would read 0.500 (250 business day observations in a year/ 500 observations over two years); on the next day it would decline to 0.498 (249/500) since the 2-year is a constant maturity point while the policy guidance was to a fixed date. Similarly for the MEP, if sales included securities with maturities as long as three years, the coverage indicator for the 4-year point would be 0.750.

provide a measure of the persistence of policies on interest rates. In contrast to announcement effects, the control measures should yield a higher degree of statistical significance, as a result of daily observations of coverage. We control for quarter and year end effects via two indicator variables. We also employ two variables to capture macroeconomic drivers of interest rates, an economic surprise index and the euro-dollar exchange rate. The economic surprise index is composed of standardized differences between economic releases and Bloomberg median forecaster values for non-farm payrolls, durable goods and retail sales. We included the euro-dollar exchange rate as a proxy for potential shocks to U.S. interest rates that may have results from European economic shocks leading to increases or decreases in dollar-denominated assets.

We supplement conventional interest rate data with two additional data sets that address (1) dealer holdings and (2) dealer sentiments. First, FRBNY releases data on Primary Dealer holdings of Treasury securities on a weekly basis.[10] Since the Primary Dealers were FRBNY's only counterparties in Treasury sales, these data provide insights into the intermediation process. With these data, we consider the effects of policies (MEP sales in particular) on Primary Dealer inventories of Treasury securities. If the sales of short-dated Treasury securities led to undesired accumulation of Treasuries, we would expect that dealer inventories would rise following each sale and then decline as dealers found buyers for the securities. Alternatively, dealers may have viewed the Federal Reserve's sales, combined with guidance on the path of future short-term interest rates, as an opportunity to lock in profits on the differences between the rate paid on Treasury securities and the cost of financing those securities. If this were the case, we would expect dealer inventories to remain stable following sales. To test for evidence of either hypothesis, we construct a test variable that rises with the number of days since the last sales operations settled. For example, if a sales operation settled on a Monday, the control would have a value of 3 as of Wednesday--the dealer would have had three days to reduce or increase the position. We control for shocks from issuance of new Treasury securities by constructing a similar variable for Treasury auctions.

Second, in addition to the Primary Dealer inventory data, we consider Primary Dealer economists' expectations of policy actions. Prior to each regularly scheduled FOMC meeting, the Federal Reserve Bank of New York (FRBNY) surveys Primary Dealers about their

---

[10] See http://www.newyorkfed.org/markets/gsds/search.html#.

expectations of policy changes and future interest rates.[11] We compare reported expectations of dealers, as opposed to more discrete {0,1} measures based only on the guidance statements. This affords us the opportunity to control for information flow effects from this policy, and from other policy and market impacts not otherwise accommodated directly in our analysis.

3.2   Methods - econometric estimation procedures

As noted earlier, previous attempts to quantify impacts of extraordinary monetary policy actions since 2007 have often employed event study techniques.[12] While MEP auctions can be characterized as "events," the effect of guidance announcements should persist throughout the sales period. To estimate impacts of these interacting programs we employ two well established protocols, a vector auto-regression with 2 lags (VAR(2)) and a Newey-West estimator with 1 lag. Beginning first with the VAR estimator we target a set of three related financing rates (Treasuries, OIS and interest rate swap rates) The three series are regressed at 1 through 5 year constant maturity points to estimate the severity of autocorrelation across series and across the curves. We employ the following estimator:

1. $$r_t = c + \hat{\beta}_1 r_{t-1} + \hat{\beta}_2 r_{t-2} + e_t$$

In the VAR(2) equation above, r is a vector that represents the nominal interest rates of each series at a particular maturity (for each of the rates in three markets at five maturity points), while $c, \hat{\beta} \& e$ represent a constant, estimated coefficients and the estimated error term, respectively. Note that these markets are highly correlated and that a meaningful proportion of market participants have the ability to shift supply or demand across maturity or instrument type.

Evidence of autocorrelation was strong enough to suggest we employ an autocorrelation robust Newey-West estimator-- our second protocol. Because we found cross-correlates of the second lag term to be much less frequently significant (the $\{i_t, j_{t-2}\}$ estimates) in these specifications, we employ just one lag. Because these short term markets feature high transaction volumes, we are not surprised to see that shocks dissipate quickly.

---

[11] See http://www.newyorkfed.org/markets/primarydealer_survey_questions.html.
[12] A notable exception is Campbell et al (2012) who employ a dynamic stochastic general equilibrium model to estimate the impact of forward guidance.

The general Newey-West estimator we employ for the weighting matrix is compact given the lag structure just described. The variance-covariance matrix, including a limited set of off-diagonal terms is:

2.
$$Var(\hat{\beta}_1) = \frac{1}{T} \sum_{l=1}^{L} \sum_{t=l+1}^{T} w_l e_t e_{t-l}(r_t r'_{t-l}),$$
$$w_l = 1 - \frac{l}{L+1}$$

The difference between $\{t,t'\}$ drives the off-diagonal terms it is limited to one lag.

As a result of observed changes in Primary Dealer inventories over the period of study, we also employ our Newey-West estimator to help us distinguish between impacts of contemporaneous policies on these inventory positions. Since we see strong statistical significance of the first lag in the VAR, we use lags of dependent variables in regressions. In all, the regressions rely on trading day observations between August 1st, 2011 and December 31st, 2012 to identify patterns of correlation across our sample.[13]

3.3   An Initial look at the Data (Univariate Measures)

Before discussing the regression results, we consider the raw data and the initial impacts of the policy announcements. Figure 1 depicts movement in the Treasury par yield curves from one to five years, from the closing before announcement to the day of policy announcement.[14]

‹ Figure 1 here ›

The gray lines in Figure 1 represent yield changes on guidance days; the black lines represent yield changes on MEP announcement days. Directional changes in yields are consistent with expectations. Guidance should work to damp the risk of holding longer maturities, and indeed guidance impacts are observed both within the period of guidance (thicker portion of gray lines) and beyond the guidance window (thinner portion). This is particularly true for the first guidance announcement where one observes a five year yield change twice the magnitude of that for the end of the guidance coverage period (roughly two years beyond the announcement date. In contrast to the guidance announcements, interest rates rose on the days of the two MEP announcements, particularly for the two and three year maturity points. Notably, the magnitude

---

[13] We have also run our primary regressions employing a Huber/White "sandwich" type estimator, though the Newey-West estimator is more efficient, the magnitudes and direction of results are stable to either method.
[14] We chose the five year point as the longest maturity in the analysis both because it is well beyond the policy announcement periods and because it is a robust pricing point in the Treasury market. In the case of the MEP, longer maturity points would also have been influenced by Federal Reserve purchases.

of the increase in rates was similar for the two and three year points even though market participants were aware that guidance almost fully covered the two year maturity but only two-thirds of the three year maturity. In both cases, the first policy announcements measure the greatest impacts (series marked with circular markers distinguish the first announcements of either program).

An interesting point from Figure 1 is that the guidance announcements, which stated the FOMC's expectations of low rates for two to three years, had pronounced effects on securities with maturities greater than the periods covered by the announcements. It is difficult to put together a story that explains these changes based solely on changes in the expected paths of short rates. While dealer survey data do help somewhat to place impacts outside the guidance window in perspective, before discussing those data, we take a moment to describe expected impacts in terms of fundamentals.

Interest rates for the shortest maturities covered by guidance should have been consistent with market views of short rates so we expect the shortest dated securities to be unaffected by this policy. For the longest dated maturity points in our sample, the guidance announcements should have affected interest rates proportional to the period affected by the announcement. For a guidance period of two years, for example, we would expect the announcement to have a more pronounced effect on 4-year yields than on 5-year yields. The market response to MEP announcements of sales of Treasury securities with three years or less to maturity, in contrast, appears consistent with expected changes: the changes in rates were largest for the maturity points most directly affected by the announcements.

While the MEP effects appear to be a direct response to a supply shock in the Treasury market, the guidance effects require fuller explanation. Guidance appears to have done more than simply alter expectations regarding the path of short-term rates over the announced period. One interpretation is that the announcements signaled a more accommodative stance by the committee rather than simply altering perceptions of the path of short term rates over guidance periods. An alternative explanation of evidence from Figure 1 is that the guidance reflected pessimistic views of the FOMC regarding the path of economic growth. This reasoning, however, seems unlikely given median FOMC member views.[15] Another interpretation is that,

---

[15] For FOMC economic projections, see http://www.federalreserve.gov/monetarypolicy/fomccalendars.htm
The central tendency of FOMC members' projections of GDP declined over 2011-2012 although very little of this decline translated into expectations of lower long-term growth.

while the guidance announcements directly affected market participants' expectations of the path of future short rates, they may have also affected investor maturity preferences and the relative premia investors are willing to pay. With either interpretation, we note that these movements are large relative to the effect directly attributable to the announcements.

The first guidance announcement signaled the path of short rates over the following two years. The second guidance announcement extended the signal by one and a half years and the third announcement added an additional half year. The announcements were writ in general terms (to "mid-year" or "year-end"), leaving room for interpretation. The interest rate changes, in terms of announcement effects, were largest for the longest maturities.

Figure 2 sheds additional light in the impact of announcements and dealer expectations. In this figure, the red lines show median dealer survey results and the interquartile range about them. Blue bars represent FOMC's anticipated period of exceptionally low federal funds rates.

<Figure 2 here>

Importantly, dealers are surveyed *before* FOMC meetings. Reading the figure with this in mind, when blue bars are above the red lines (as with the first guidance announcement) the FOMC's stated period before an increase in federal funds target rate exceeded the median of primary dealers' stated expectation of the first increase in the federal funds target.. Thus these survey data suggest that one reason the first guidance statement was observably larger (in Figure 1) was that FOMC surprised dealers, whereas in the following two guidance announcements, the FOMC supported contemporaneous expectations. Since dealer surveys might be dismissed as "cheap talk", showing dealer preferences rather than expectations, we look at dealer positions in Treasuries. Before looking at those data however we take a moment to consider the MEP in context.

The two MEP announcements were of significantly different size. The first promised sales of $400 billion in Treasury securities with short maturities while the second was smaller ($270 billion) and offered no hope of expansion since, by program completion, the Federal Reserve's holdings of short-dated securities would be near zero. While the initial yield changes on announcement days appear similar to the guidance announcements, the decline in yield responses from one announcement to the next is consistent with a straight-forward explanation of a smaller supply shock although it is also consistent with less surprise about the second MEP program since it represented a continuation of the first program.

Over 2011-2012, dealers increased their inventories of Treasury securities and, in particular, Treasuries in the maturity range sold by the Federal Reserve through MEP sales. The Federal Reserve Bank of New York publishes the positions of its Primary Dealer counterparties on a weekly basis.[16] Positions are listed by asset type and, for Treasury securities, by maturity. One maturity coincidentally and conveniently overlaps almost perfectly with MEP sales. Figure 3 offers a look at how inventories of bills, short notes (less than 3 years to maturity), and the longer MEP offerings (3-6 years to maturity) evolved over the period of study.

<Figure 3 here>

Changes in holdings appear consistent with dealers' profit expectations: bills, with their low returns, were relatively unattractive regardless of FOMC actions while short-dated notes offered positive returns that, with FOMC actions, generated little price risk. The FOMC rate guidance extending, at most out to 3½ years, however, offered only a modest reduction in price risk for 3-6 year investments.

While changes in holdings *appear* consistent with interest in a relatively risk-free return given interest rate guidance, it is also possible that dealers held the securities because demand for Treasury securities was to some or other degree sated. We seek to determine which of these possible explanations is most likely in our discussion of results from regression analysis.

4.0 Analysis of the Data

The announcement effects shown in Figure 1 suggest re-pricing was caused by the policy statements released by the Federal Reserve, but the raw data have obvious shortcomings. Identifying the price response to announcements, net of other impacts requires an identification strategy. Because announcements may be anticipated such a strategy should include any proportion of the price response that occurred prior to the announcement. Anticipation can occur either because some market participants are prescient or because policymakers re-set expectations through speeches prior to the announcement. We isolate announcement effects from other contemporaneous events that may have influenced prices by employing prices from related markets as controls and we create a set of indicators based on the maturity boundaries set by the policies. We then broaden the analyses to dealer inventory positions.

---

[16] The positions are reported as of each Wednesday with an eight day lag, see http://www.newyorkfed.org/markets/gsds/search.cfm.

We analyze the results of three sets of regressions; one where the dependent variable is the daily change in Treasury zero coupon constant maturity rates, a second where the dependent variable is the spreads of those rates to overnight index swaps (OIS), and a third where the dependent variable is the spread between the zero coupon Treasury yield and interest rate swap rates.

4.1 Regressions devoted Treasury Yields

In this section we estimate equation 2 using the Newey-West estimator described in Section 3.2. The regression results for the one to five year constant maturity series are presented in Table 3. The regressors include announcement effects, coverage effects and the controls described in Section 3.1. To run analyses that treat coverage and other phenomenon consistently, we employ the same regressors to analyze potential impacts for Treasury-OIS spreads and Treasury-swap spreads. The spreads to OIS are shown as indicators of the policy effects on the path of overnight rates embodied in the OIS rates. The spreads are shown to measure possible transmission effects over proximate markets.

<Table 3 here>

Beginning with yields (columns in bold), guidance announcements had increasingly large effects on Treasury rates, moving along the yield curve from 1.5 basis points on 1-year yields to 10.6 basis points on the 5-year yield.[17] This is remarkable given that each of the guidance announcements extended the period of likely low overnight rates by two years or less. In addition, it is likely that investors generally did not expect meaningful increases in federal funds rates within the next year or so at the time the initial date-based guidance was issued (by Figure 2, the primary dealer surveys conducted by FRBNY in June and August of 2011, just ahead of the guidance announcement reports median expectations of 5 quarters until any such tightening would occur). Consequently, we would have expected that the most pronounced effects from guidance announcements would have emerged around 2-year yields.

---

[17] Moessner (2013) also finds that the effects of guidance announcements were larger for Treasury and Eurodollar rates beyond the stated guidance periods.

The MEP program announcements generally increase yields in line with expected supply effects. Estimated magnitudes of impact are greatest in the 2-3 year range, at roughly four basis points. A constant and the lagged dependent variable are included in all specifications.[18]

The coverage effect is only significant for the MEP which is not surprising given the market response to the guidance announcements. For Treasury yields, the MEP coverage effect was only significant at the 1-year and 2-year maturity points which were fully covered by the program throughout its life. The effect of increased MEP coverage on yields is small, roughly 0.7 basis points, but provides statistical evidence of persistence for policy's effects on yields.

The spreads between Treasury yields and swaps narrowed with guidance announcements and widened with the MEP announcements. The guidance announcements reduced all short-dated rates but the effects were larger for the OIS market than the swaps market while, on the MEP announcements, OIS rates moved parallel to Treasury rates, leaving spreads unchanged. In contrast, MEP announcements had no effect on swap rates, leading to a widening of spreads. Coverage effects for guidance were small and generally statistically insignificant. The MEP coverage effects, however, were negative and statistically significant for the longer maturity points. That is, Treasury yields relative to OIS or swaps remained higher indicating persistence of supply effects.

Comparing the two spreads, the swap spreads were generally insignificant implying that the changes in swap rates were in the same direction as the changes in Treasury rates and of roughly the same magnitude. The one caveat here is with regard to coverage of MEP. Recall that the swap rates are based on interbank lending costs while the OIS is based on the Federal Reserve's targeted overnight rate. Note the contrast between OIS, which directly reflects views of the path of the overnight policy rate, and swap rates, which moved in tandem with Treasury rates on policy announcement days.

While announcement effects were negligible for swap rates, the policy coverage indicators suggest MEP had a lasting effect on rates over time. Swap yields were, on average, one to seven basis points wider over the sales period with the largest effects for the longest maturities. Figure 4 places relative impacts in perspective.

<Figure 4 here>

---

[18] In contrast when we introduce a general control for FOMC announcements, the general FOMC indicator is not statistically significant: notably neither the direction nor magnitude of estimated guidance and MEP effects are altered. These results are available from the authors by request.

Guidance announcement effects, shown in first panel, have negative impacts on Treasury yields. The estimated positive impacts for MEP announcements in the second panel have roughly equal magnitude as the guidance announcements at the 2-year maturity. A good question is why any MEP effect should be observed. The overall supply impact of MEP was zero, and the FOMC had provided guidance on path of short rates. To answer the question, we need an explanation that relies on the MEP affecting term premia through sectorspecific maturity preferences (in the spirit of a set of Vayanos-Vila type of preferred habitat investors coexisting with capital constrained arbitrageurs) or transaction costs associated with portfolio adjustments. Either one of these would explain the increase in yields associated with the MEP announcements (as seen in figures 1 and 4).

4.2   Dealer Positions

In Figure 3, we compared positions in the MEP sales maturity range to those of the adjacent maturity buckets (covering bills and securities with maturities from three to six years). Dealer positions within the MEP sales maturities rose rapidly through the program while positions in the adjacent maturity buckets were relatively stable. Unlike shocks caused by U.S. Treasury issuance of new securities, Federal Reserve supply injections were spread across a relatively large number of securities, with some uncertainty about supply of individual securities entering the market, because the Federal Reserve offered a range of securities in each sales operation with the amounts sold dependent on quantities and prices bid.

One possible explanation for this rise in positions is that the Federal Reserve's counterparties were unable to distribute securities they received in the MEP sales operations expediently. Another is that dealers held the inventories willingly—seeing the sales as an arbitrage opportunity since they coincided with guidance that short rates would not increase.

These two possible explanations have very different implications for the growth of dealer positions. If dealers had difficulty distributing the MEP sales awards, we would expect dealer positions to decline following the settlement of sales operations--they would distribute them, albeit more slowly. If instead the growth in dealer positions was a perceived arbitrage based on guidance policy, we would expect dealer positions to rise with settlement of sales operations and show no additional trend following settlement. An additional implication of dealer arbitrage would be that positions would rise most for the securities with strongest potential for arbitrage profits -- those with maturities within the policy guidance period.[19]

To test for evidence of either of these explanations we build a variable of the number of days between the last settlement date of MEP sales and the dealer reporting date. So, for example, if a MEP sales operation settled on a Monday then given a Wednesday close of business reporting date, our indicator would record a value of "3" since the dealers would have had Monday, Tuesday and Wednesday in which to reduce their positions. If dealers had trouble reducing their positions in MEP securities, we would expect this indicator to have a negative value. Table 4 offers results from these regressions. Since the dealers were also faced with regular supply from new Treasury issuance, we created similar controls for monthly auctions of 2-year, 3-year, and 5-year securities by the Treasury.

<Table 4 here>

Columns 1-3 utilize dealer positions, while columns 4-6 use the change in dealer positions as the dependent variable. Dealer positions are reported weekly. As a result of the switch to weekly frequency, reported sample size is much lower than it was for the pricing data though these data cover the same period of analysis as for Table 3.

Beginning with the bills column there are no strongly significant results (MEP sales did not include the sales of Treasury bills). The weakly significant result regarding accumulating dealer positions in the days following MEP auctions (column 1, from settlement to report), fails to be supported by column 4. Generally these results are in line with the modest trend in accumulation over the period shown in Figure 3.

We move next to columns 2 and 5, regarding Treasury coupon securities with remaining maturities less than 3 years. In column 2, we find that longer time periods between Treasury 2-3 year note auctions or Federal Reserve MEP auctions are associated with greater accumulations of dealer positions; implying that the dealers did not reduce their positions over time. The result in column 2 with respect to Treasury auctions of 5 years is consistent with dealers actively substituting maturities covered by guidance for those outside of it. Moving to column 5 we find that time since Treasury auctions is strongly correlated with changes in dealer positions; however the Fed's MEP sales are not. The same lack of robustness can be found in the

---

[19] Other indicators such as trading volumes, or bid-ask spreads do not suggest a lack of liquidity over this period.

relationship of Treasury 5-year issuance, though the coefficients are consistent with column 2 in terms of direction (sign).

Finally looking at dealer positions in notes from the 3-6 year range, in column 3 we find that while MEP sales bear no robust correlation with inventories, there are strong positive correlations with Treasury issuance in the shorter and longer MEP covered notes categories, lending support overall to a partial coverage thesis. Of particular interest, Treasury issuance in the 2-3 year category is positively correlated with increases in dealer 3-6 year inventories as well. The same general results are found with respect to changes in dealer positions (column 6). Overall these results suggest that dealers willingly accumulated positions in short notes covered by the guidance.

4.3   Dealer Expectations Revisited

In the preceding analyses, we have implicitly assumed that market participants' expectations were consistent with the policy guidance provided by the Federal Reserve. Recall from discussion earlier that Figure 2 plots reported dealer expectations and the FOMC's anticipated period of extraordinarily low rates. Taken literally, Figure 2 suggests that dealers' expectations for the end of monetary accommodation steadily moved out over 2011 and 2012, with the median expectation of the first increase in the fed funds target moving from late 2012 in August 2011 to late 2015 by September 2012. In terms of FOMC announcement impacts, we interpret the first announcement, in August of 2011 as increasing dealer stated expectations from five to nine quarters. Following the first announcement, subsequent guidance statements did little to influence dealer stated expectations.[20]

5.0   Conclusions

The implicit MEP policy trade-off was that the positive effects on the economy from purchasing long-dated Treasuries would more than offset the negative effects on the economy of selling short-dated Treasuries. In the absence of guidance, this trade-off could work either because the market for short-dated Treasuries is much deeper than for long-dated Treasuries or because the economy is more responsive to changes in long rates than short rates. Date-based guidance

---

[20] While it looks as if FOMC guidance is consistently under median dealer expectations, announcements always state expectations of rates staying at the 0-0.25 percent range to "at least" the announced date.

created an additional mechanism for this trade-off to work by suppressing the effects of sales on short-dated Treasuries. Across our three data sets covering pricing, dealer holdings, and dealer expectations, we see evidence that the guidance was effective in lowering the implied path of the federal funds rate. Dealer expectations, as expressed by changes in market rates or by responses to survey questions, shifted; dealer inventory accumulations further suggest a willingness to support those expectations with investment in Treasury securities.

Our findings suggest that the MEP did raise rates modestly at the short end of the curve and that the increases were not significantly different for the sales of securities within the guidance windows than they were for securities with maturities that extend beyond the guidance windows, suggesting a high degree of substitutability within the relatively narrow maturity range that we examined. Similarly, market participants did not distinguish between maturities within and outside of the guidance period.

Assuming the date-based guidance was viewed by market participants as a commitment to the path of short rates, the increases in rates associated with the MEP sales provide evidence that yields are composed of more than the arbitrage-free rate of return. The increase in yields on MEP announcements in the presence of guidance provides support for the preferred habitat or term premium approaches put forth by other authors.

Bibliography

Bauer, Michael D. and Glenn D. Rudebusch (2012). "The Signaling Channel for Federal Reserve Bond Purchases" Federal Reserve Bank of San Francisco Working Paper Series 2011-21.

Campbell, Jeffrey R., Charles L. Evans, Jonas D.M. Fisher and Alejandro Justiniano (2012). "Macroeconomic Effects of Federal Reserve Forward Guidance." *Brookings Papers on Economic Activity*, Spring 2012.

D'Amico, Stefania and Thomas King (2012). "Flow and Stock Effects of Large-Scale Treasury Purchases" *Journal of Financial Economics*, 2013, 108(2): 425-48.

Gagnon, Joseph, Matthew Raskin, Julie Remache and Brian Sack (2011). "The Financial Market Effects of the Federal Reserve's Large-Scale Asset Purchases" *International Journal of Central Banking* 7 (1) March 2011.

Greene, William H. (2003) *Econometric Analysis*, fifth edition. Prentice Hall, NJ

Gurkaynak, Refet S., Brian Sack, and Jonathan H. Wright (2007). "The U.S. Treasury Yield Curve: 1961 to the Present" *Journal of Monetary Economics* 54(8) pp 2291-2304.

Hamilton, James and Cynthia Wu (2012). "The Effectiveness of Alternative Monetary Policy Tools in a Zero Lower Bound Environment" *Journal of Money, Credit, and Banking* 44 (1), pp 3-46.

Hrung, Warren B. and Jason S. Seligman (2011). "Responses to the Financial Crisis, Treasury Debt, and the Impact on Short-Term Money Markets" *NYFRB Staff Reports* 481, January.

Li, Canlin and Min Wei (2012). "Term Structure Modelling with Supply Factors and the Federal Reserve's Large Scale Asset Purchase Programs" Federal Reserve Board Working Paper (2012-37).

Krishnamurthy, Arvind and Annette Vissing-Jorgensen (2011). "The Effects of Quantitative Easing on Interest Rates" *Brookings Papers on Economic Activity*, fall.

Modigliani, F., and Merton H. Miller (1958). "The Cost of Capital, Corporate Finance and the Theory of Investment." *American Economic Review*, 48, 261-97

Moessner, Richhild (2013). "Effects of explicit FOMC policy rate guidance on market interest rates" De Nederlandsche Bank, 384, July 2013.

Rudebusch, Glenn D., and John C. Williams. (2008). "Revealing the Secrets of the Temple: The Value of Publishing Central Bank Interest Rate Projections." In *Asset Prices and Monetary Policy*, edited by J. Y. Campbell. University of Chicago Press.

Vayanos, Dimitri and Jean-Luc Vila (2009). "A Preferred-Habitat Model of the Term Structure of Interest Rates" *NBER working paper series* 15487.

Woodford, Michael (2012). "Methods of Policy Accommodation at the Interest-Rate Lower Bound" Working Paper, available via Columbia University, NY.

Table 1: Characterization of Hypotheses -- General predicted Effects of Programs

Directional Pressures on Short-Dated Treasury Security Rates

Announce Date	Mid-2013	End-2014	Mid-2015	Beginning-2016
8/9/2011 gu	↓			
9/21/2011 mep	↓	↑	↑	
1/25/2012 gu	↓	↓	↑	
6/20/2012 mep	↓	↓	↑	↑
9/13/2012 gu	↓	↓	↓	↑

Arrows reflect assumption that rate guidance dominates supply pressures

Table 2: Summary Statistics

	# Obs	Mean	Std. Dev.	Min	Max
Dependent Variables					
Treasury zero coupon yield estimates - 1 yr	355	0.1946	0.0377	0.0967	0.2790
Treasury zero coupon yield estimates - 2 yr	355	0.2641	0.0450	0.1583	0.4275
Treasury zero coupon yield estimates - 3 yr	355	0.4176	0.0683	0.3025	0.6762
Treasury zero coupon yield estimates - 4 yr	355	0.6216	0.1051	0.4313	0.9587
Treasury zero coupon yield estimates - 5 yr	355	0.8518	0.1453	0.5886	1.3170
Treasury - OIS Spread - 1 yr	355	-0.0615	0.0172	-0.1050	-0.0106
Treasury - OIS Spread - 2 yr	355	-0.0948	0.0198	-0.1730	-0.0394
Treasury - OIS Spread - 3 yr	355	-0.1375	0.0225	-0.2076	-0.0550
Treasury - OIS Spread - 4 yr	355	-0.1412	0.0232	-0.2016	-0.0146
Treasury - OIS Spread - 5 yr	355	-0.1338	0.0287	-0.2010	0.0341
Treasury - ED Spread - 1 yr	354	0.2888	0.1259	0.0830	0.6190
Treasury - ED Spread - 2 yr	354	0.2684	0.1073	0.0802	0.5526
Treasury - ED Spread - 3 yr	354	0.2279	0.0964	0.0463	0.4850
Treasury - ED Spread - 4 yr	354	0.2196	0.0983	0.0262	0.5069
Treasury - ED Spread - 5 yr	354	0.2221	0.0972	0.0186	0.5516
Policy Coverage Ratios (Controls)					
guidance announcement impact - 1yr	355	0.9831	0.1291	0.0000	1.0000
guidance announcement impact - 2yr	355	0.9297	0.1496	0.0000	1.0000
guidance announcement impact - 3yr	355	0.7987	0.2259	0.0000	1.1300
guidance announcement impact - 4yr	355	0.5990	0.1693	0.0000	0.8500
guidance announcement impact - 5yr	355	0.4792	0.1356	0.0000	0.6800
MEP announcement impact - 1yr	355	0.8986	0.3023	0.0000	1.0000
MEP announcement impact - 2yr	355	0.8986	0.3023	0.0000	1.0000
MEP announcement impact - 3yr	355	0.8986	0.3023	0.0000	1.0000
MEP announcement impact - 4yr	355	0.7375	0.2533	0.0000	0.9000
MEP announcement impact - 5yr	355	0.5901	0.2027	0.0000	0.7200
Standard Time Considerations (Controls)					
quarter end dummy	355	0.0169	0.1291	0.0000	1.0000
year end dummy	355	0.0056	0.0750	0.0000	1.0000

Table 3: Time Series Regression – Policy Impacts on selected points on the US Treasury Yield Curve and two related spreads

maturity:	1yr			2yr			3yr			4yr			5yr		
	yield	spreads		yield	spreads		yield	spreads		yield	spreads		yield	spreads	
		OIS	swap		OIS	swap		OIS	swap		OIS	swap		OIS	swap
Policy Variables:															
guidance announcements	-0.0159**	0.00946*	0.00303	-0.0488**	0.0232***	0.00459	-0.0758***	0.0257*	0.00754	-0.0931***	0.0313*	0.0179	-0.103***	0.0435	0.0172
	(0.00768)	(0.00535)	(0.00843)	(0.0191)	(0.00867)	(0.0151)	(0.0262)	(0.0137)	(0.0271)	(0.0310)	(0.0189)	(0.0353)	(0.0343)	(0.0303)	(0.0355)
MEP announcements	0.0259***	-0.0102***	-0.0251***	0.0416***	-0.0227***	-0.0229	0.0390***	-0.0292**	-0.0254	0.0377***	-0.0262	-0.0612	0.0246***	-0.0139	-0.00508
	(0.000998)	(0.00232)	(0.00614)	(0.00780)	(0.00713)	(0.0180)	(0.00488)	(0.0143)	(0.0202)	(0.00648)	(0.0185)	(0.0108)	(0.00425)	(0.0189)	(0.00991)
coverage of guidance	-0.00111	0.0124***	0.0140	0.00783	-0.00199	0.0105	0.0109	0.00511	0.00281	0.00899	0.00564	-0.00142	0.00562	-0.000836	-0.0135
	(0.00915)	(0.00467)	(0.0108)	(0.00612)	(0.00375)	(0.0102)	(0.00941)	(0.00576)	(0.0125)	(0.0177)	(0.0104)	(0.0215)	(0.0280)	(0.0136)	(0.0325)
coverage of MEP	0.00706***	-0.000152	0.0107**	0.0115***	-0.00481*	0.0187***	0.0171***	-0.0108***	0.0285***	0.0307**	-0.0218***	0.0468***	0.0497**	-0.0357***	0.0683***
	(0.00259)	(0.00217)	(0.00499)	(0.00399)	(0.00260)	(0.00626)	(0.00659)	(0.00358)	(0.0101)	(0.0122)	(0.00599)	(0.0152)	(0.0192)	(0.00884)	(0.0214)
Control Variables:															
economic surprise	0.000176	0.000226	0.000718	0.00179	-0.00246	0.000287	0.00235	-0.00187	-0.00207	0.00298	-0.00654**	-0.00128	0.00363	-0.00914**	0.00137
	(0.00331)	(0.00319)	(0.00496)	(0.00553)	(0.00318)	(0.00588)	(0.00821)	(0.00429)	(0.00722)	(0.0107)	(0.00331)	(0.0102)	(0.0127)	(0.00401)	(0.0114)
euro	-0.00768	-0.0101	-0.0207	0.0252	-0.0165	-0.0105	0.0593	-0.0447**	0.0216	0.148**	-0.0824***	0.107*	0.237***	-0.125***	0.192**
	(0.0176)	(0.0163)	(0.0333)	(0.0241)	(0.0136)	(0.0328)	(0.0422)	(0.0190)	(0.0376)	(0.0683)	(0.0277)	(0.0558)	(0.0909)	(0.0331)	(0.0748)
lagged dependent	0.849***	0.529***	0.937***	0.906***	0.799***	0.931***	0.897***	0.732***	0.909***	0.885***	0.592***	0.893***	0.876***	0.510***	0.878***
	(0.0263)	(0.0574)	(0.0254)	(0.0225)	(0.0379)	(0.0221)	(0.0253)	(0.0453)	(0.0236)	(0.0282)	(0.0565)	(0.0275)	(0.0295)	(0.0682)	(0.0309)
quarter end	0.000444	-0.00253	-0.0125**	-0.00519	0.00239	-0.0138*	-0.00546	0.00575	-0.0101	-0.00331	0.0191*	-0.0121	0.000204	0.0180	-0.0158
	(0.00525)	(0.00387)	(0.00594)	(0.00640)	(0.00216)	(0.00762)	(0.00855)	(0.00453)	(0.00827)	(0.0106)	(0.0110)	(0.00973)	(0.0128)	(0.0118)	(0.00964)
Constant	0.0255	-0.0105	0.0604	-0.0238	0.00455	0.0537	-0.0435	0.0240	0.0427	-0.130	0.0734*	-0.0328	-0.210*	0.147***	-0.0941
	(0.0292)	(0.0239)	(0.0599)	(0.0361)	(0.0194)	(0.0572)	(0.0586)	(0.0274)	(0.0563)	(0.0898)	(0.0380)	(0.0717)	(0.115)	(0.0460)	(0.0872)
Observations	355	355	353	355	355	353	355	355	353	355	355	353	355	355	353

Note: standard errors in parentheses -- (***p<0.01, **p<0.05, *p<0.1)

Table 4: Evolution of Dealer Inventory Positions

VARIABLES	DEALER POSITIONS				CHANGE IN DEALER POSITIONS			
	(1) Bills	(2) Notes <3 yrs	(3) Notes 3-6 yrs		(4) Bills	(5) Notes <3 yrs	(6) Notes 3-6 yrs	
US Treasury issuance 2-3 yrs	488.3	1,689***	563.5***		304.7	1,277***	688.3***	
days since most recent settlement	(383.1)	(326.3)	(164.9)		(552.1)	(360.8)	(195.4)	
US Treasury issuance 5 yrs	-85.74	-458.3**	331.9***		-11.41	-314.0	310.7**	
days since most recent settlement	(205.8)	(190.6)	(82.91)		(271.1)	(221.1)	(136.4)	
Federal Reserve MEP sales	821.7*	921.3**	62.12		98.77	197.0	414.5	
days since most recent settlement	(432.8)	(389.9)	(243.1)		(513.3)	(456.3)	(321.2)	
lagged dependent variable	0.483***	0.902***	0.964***		-0.326***	-0.297***	-0.0482	
	(0.0990)	(0.0358)	(0.0346)		(0.109)	(0.0847)	(0.0840)	
Constant	8,396***	-2,225	-6,841***		-380.8	-2,369	-8,959***	
	(3,029)	(2,749)	(1,177)		(3,561)	(2,614)	(1,850)	
Observations (weekly)	108	108	108		107	107	107	

*Standard errors in parentheses: ***p<0.01, **p<0.05, *p<0.1*

Figure I: Observed Changes in Yields over the short-end of the US Treasury Yield Curve Following Policy Announcements

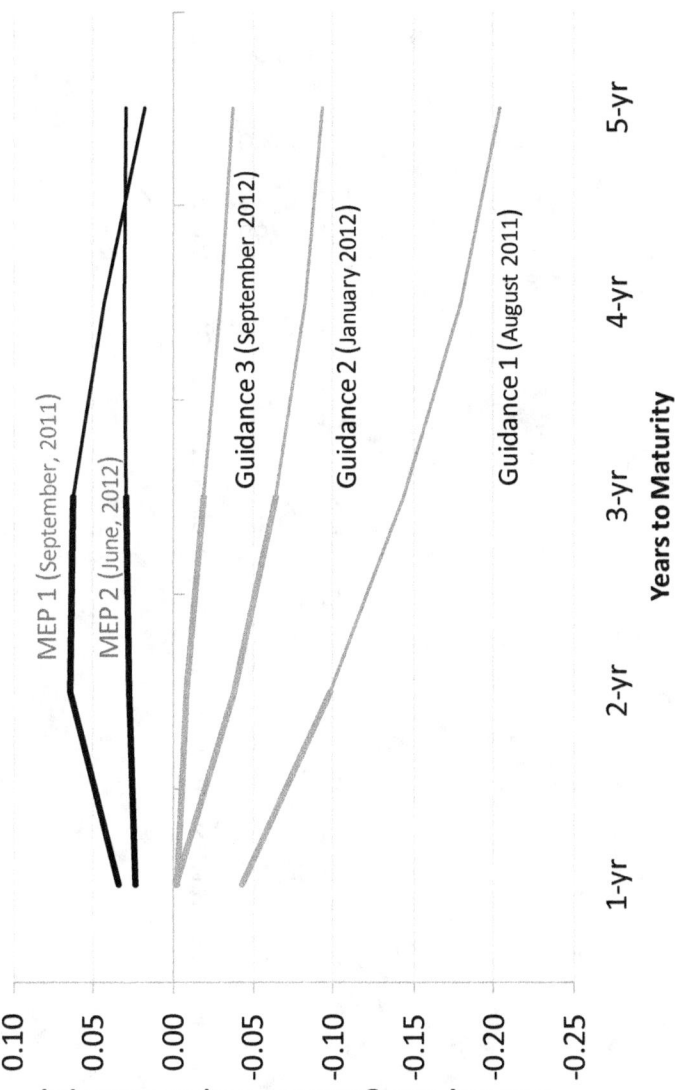

Figure 2: FOMC Interest Rate Guidance and Dealer Expectations of Initial Interest Rate Hikes

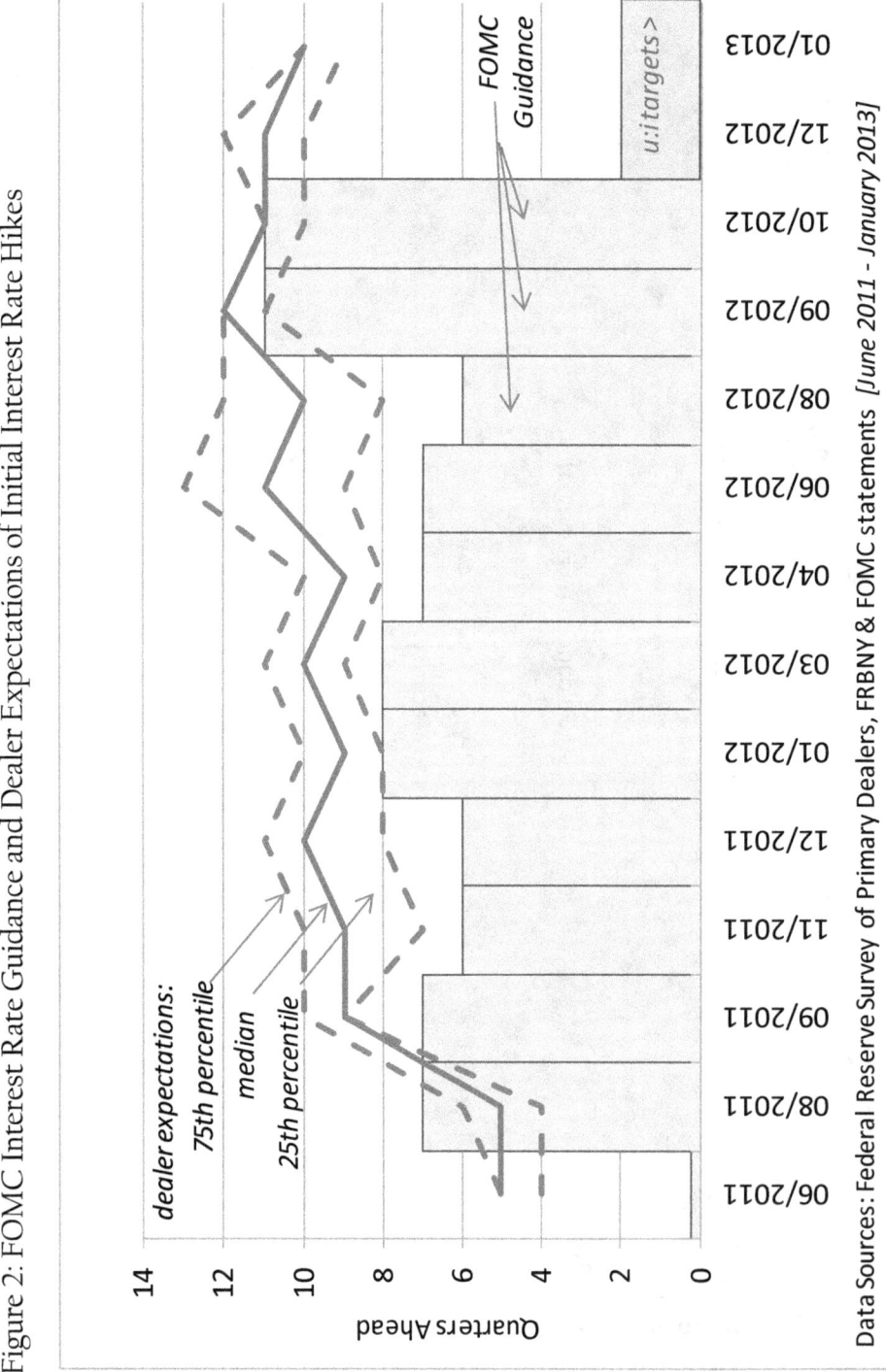

Data Sources: Federal Reserve Survey of Primary Dealers, FRBNY & FOMC statements [June 2011 - January 2013]

Figure 3: Dealer Inventory Positions in US Treasury Bills and Notes over the Policy Analysis Period

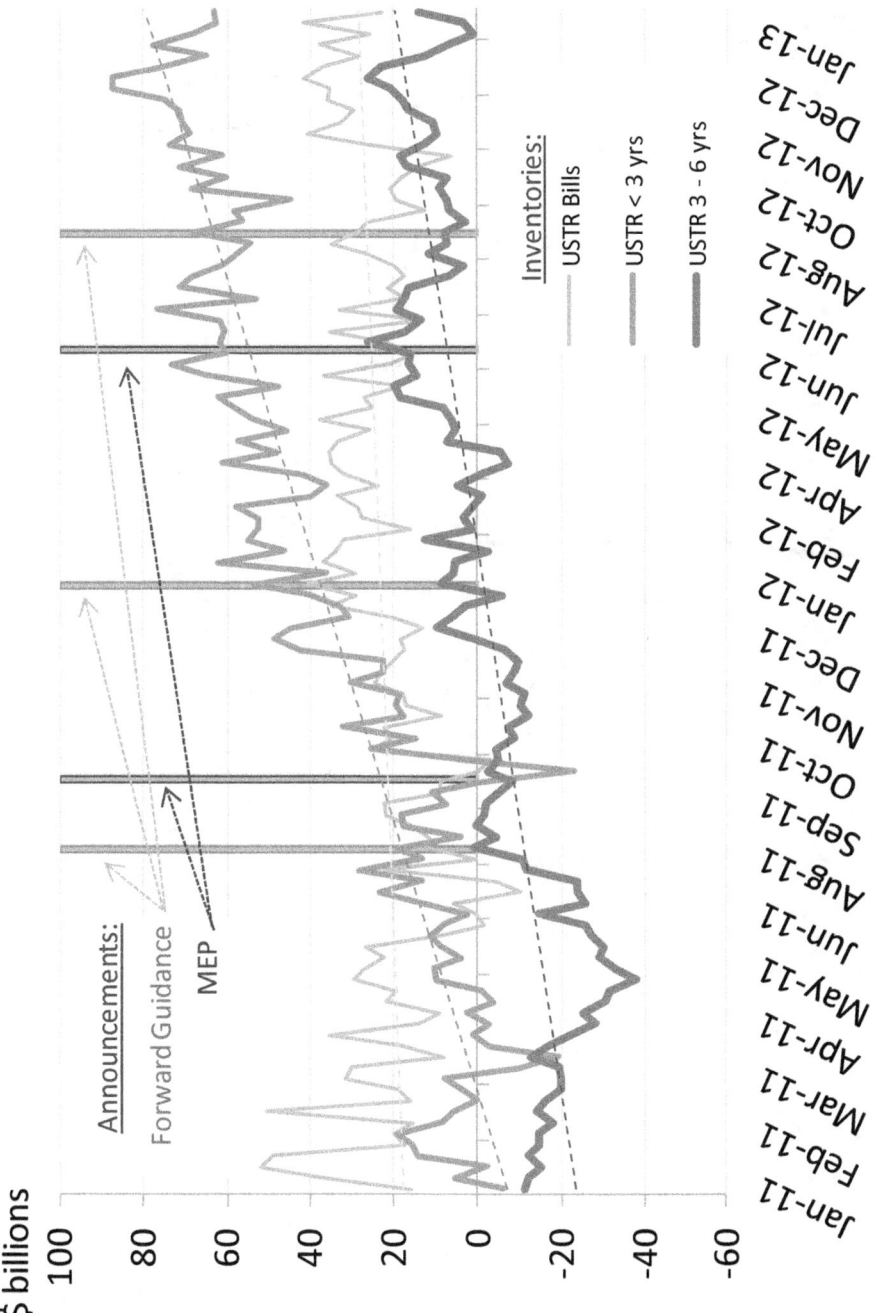

Figure 4: Estimated FOMC guidance & MEP announcement effects (coefficients)

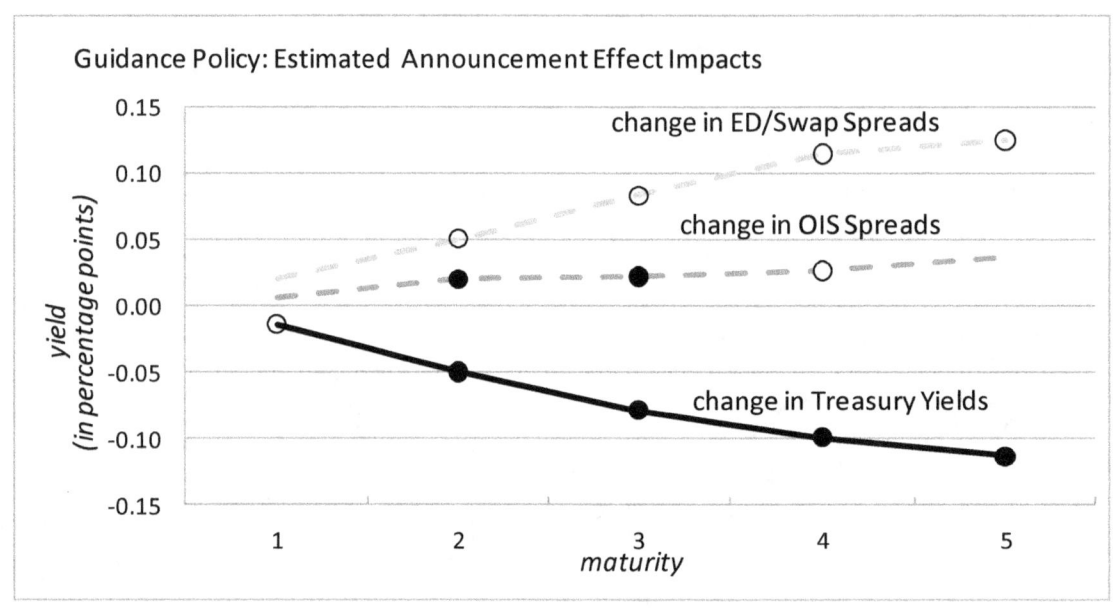

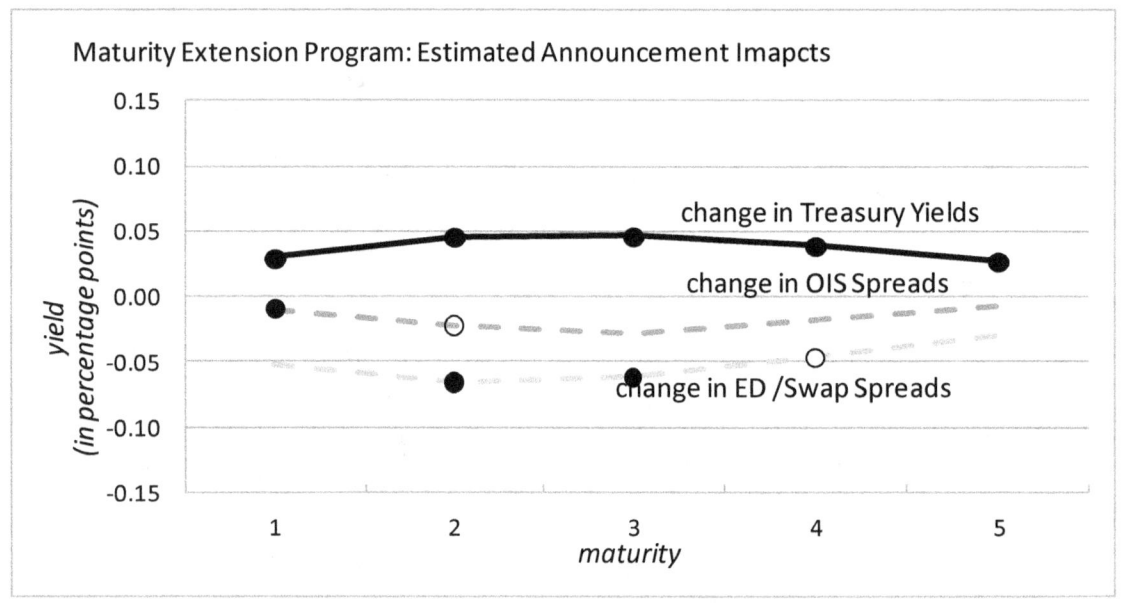

www.ingramcontent.com/pod-product-compliance
Lightning Source LLC
Chambersburg PA
CBHW081819170526
45167CB00008B/3461